Andy and The Friendship Puzzle:
A Story About Making Friends When You Have ADHD

Written By Sharika Pruitt
Illustrated By Saad Malik

Dedicated to my Beautiful Neurodivergent Daughter Mackynzie, I love you and thank you for helping me be an expert on this topic.

Table of Contents

Chapter 1: Meet Andy

I'm Andy, an 8-year-old bursting with energy. My days are like vibrant whirlwinds of excitement and curiosity. I have this big, bright smile that can light up a room, but there's something about me that makes connecting with others a bit tricky—I've got ADHD.

Every day at school, I fidget in my chair, unable to sit still during lessons. My mind races a hundred miles per hour, and sometimes, I can't help but blurt out answers or jump up when I'm supposed to stay seated. Even though I'm super creative and love learning, making friends is a puzzle I can't seem to solve.

I watch other kids play games and form groups effortlessly on the playground. I long to join in, but the constant movement and distractions make it hard to find my place in the group dynamics. Some of my classmates don't understand why I act the way I do, making them keep their distance.

Sitting alone on a bench one sunny afternoon, I spot something shiny on the ground. It's a peculiar puzzle piece, unlike any I've seen before. It has vibrant colors and beckons me. I pick it up, feeling a strange connection to this small, mysterious object.

As I examine the puzzle piece, I wonder if it holds the key to the friendship puzzle, I desperately want to solve. With determination in my eyes, I decide that this puzzle piece will be the beginning of a grand adventure to find true friendship, even if it means facing the challenges of my ADHD head-on.

And so, my journey to unlock the secrets of friendship begins, with the shiny puzzle piece as my guide and a heart full of hope. Little do I know that this adventure will lead to unexpected discoveries, unique friendships, and a celebration of the extraordinary qualities that make me who I am.

Chapter 2: The Mysterious Puzzle Piece

Carrying the shiny puzzle piece everywhere, it became my secret buddy, like a little whispering friend promising awesome things about friendship. I wondered where this magical puzzle piece came from and what cool things it could do.

One day after school, I thought of sharing my discovery with Mrs. Jenkins, my favorite teacher. She's always so lovely and gets me. Holding the puzzle piece in my hands, I approached her desk.

"Mrs. Jenkins," I said, a mix of excitement and nervousness in my voice, "I found this super cool puzzle piece, and I think it's the key to making friends. But I don't know where it came from or what to do with it."

Mrs. Jenkins smiled warmly, inviting me to sit beside her. She checked out the puzzle piece with genuine interest, her eyes lighting up with curiosity. "Andy, sometimes, the most amazing things come into our lives to teach us important stuff. Let's go on this adventure together and see where it takes us."

So, Mrs. Jenkins and I began our quest to figure out the puzzle piece's secrets. We read about friendship, explored books on teamwork, and even got a school counselor to join us. It was like going on a super cool mission, and I was learning lots of essential things about how people connect and become friends.

The puzzle piece sparked with approval as I soaked up all these new ideas. With every discovery, I felt stronger and more in control. That puzzle piece was more than just a thing; it was like a symbol of hope, showing me, I could make friends and understand people better.

Eager to share my newfound wisdom, I invited some classmates to join me on this incredible journey. With their own puzzle pieces, we formed a team, ready for whatever came our way. Standing together, each with a piece of the friendship puzzle, we felt like a team, ready for exciting adventures and the joy of true friendship. Little did we know that our adventure was beginning, and those puzzle pieces would guide us through challenges, laughter, and the real magic of friendship.

Chapter 3: The Puzzle Hunt

Feeling all pumped up with our cool puzzle pieces, I decided it was time to embark on a quest to find more of these fantastic pieces and solve the friendship puzzle once and for all. So, together with my new friends, we set off on what felt like the most exciting adventure ever.

Our first stop was the school library. Mrs. Jenkins mentioned that books are like treasure chests full of knowledge and might hold clues about finding more puzzle pieces. We combed through the shelves, picking out books about teamwork, understanding differences, and making friends.
One book had a map of the school garden, and we thought, "Hey, maybe there's a puzzle piece hidden there!" We dashed outside, our eyes scanning the area like detectives on a mission. After digging around (not literally with shovels, just looking around the area), we found a shiny puzzle piece near the big oak tree. Success!

Excitement bubbled up as we continued our puzzle hunt. The next clue led us to the art room. We thought, "Hmm, maybe there's a puzzle piece in all this creativity!" As we explored the art supplies, brushes, and paints, we stumbled upon another piece hidden in a box of colorful markers. Double success

The group grew closer with every puzzle piece we found, and it felt like we were building something super special. Like every friend, each piece had a unique design and was different but equally awesome.

Our puzzle hunt took us to the playground, the cafeteria, and the music room. We laughed, shared stories, and high-fived each other for every new discovery. It was like a giant puzzle party; we were the puzzle-solving champions!

As the day went on, we realized that the puzzle pieces weren't just leading us to friendship but also teaching us essential stuff. We learned about cooperation, patience, and the joy of working together.

With our pockets full of puzzle pieces and hearts full of friendship, we returned to class feeling like we'd just uncovered the first chapters of the greatest adventure ever. Little did we know that more challenges, surprises, and amazing friendships awaited us as we continued our quest to complete the friendship puzzle.

Chapter 4: A Friend in Need

So, there we were, our pockets filled with sparkly puzzle pieces, feeling like a team of friendship explorers. As we returned to class, I noticed Jake, one of my classmates, looking down. He struggled with a tricky math problem, and everyone seemed too busy to help.

That's when I thought, "Hey, maybe our puzzle pieces can help in more ways than one!" I walked over to Jake and said, "Hey, Jake! Need a hand with that math problem?" He looked surprised but smiled and said, "Yeah, I could use some help."
I sat down beside him, and we tackled the problem together. Using the teamwork, we'd learned on our puzzle hunt, Jake and I made math feel like a fun puzzle to solve. We laughed and high-fived, and before we knew it, the problem wasn't so tricky anymore.

Other kids in the class noticed what we were doing, and soon, a few more joined in. It was like a teamwork party, and we were all helping each other. The classroom buzzed with positive energy and being part of something so cool felt incredible.

When the teacher saw what was happening, she smiled and said, "Looks like our classroom is turning into a friendship workshop!" That's when it hit me – our puzzle pieces weren't just about finding friends; they were about helping each other and making a difference.

After class, Jake approached me and said, "Thanks, Andy. I never thought math could be that much fun!" I grinned and replied, "No problem, Jake! Teamwork makes everything better."

Helping a friend was like adding another piece to our friendship puzzle. Each act of kindness brought us closer together, strengthening our bond. As we left the classroom that day, I felt a warm glow, knowing that our puzzle pieces weren't just connecting us; they were creating a web of incredible friendships.

Little did I know that our next puzzle adventure would be even more exciting, filled with surprises, laughter, and the discovery that friendship is about what you gain and give.

Chapter 5: Friendship Workshop

The next day, something super cool happened – our teacher, Mrs. Jenkins, turned our classroom into a Friendship Workshop. I didn't even know that was a thing, but it sounded fantastic! She explained that we would learn more about understanding and being even better friends.

Mrs. Jenkins started by asking us to share our favorite things about ourselves. It was like show-and-tell, but instead of bringing in stuff, we got to talk about what made us unique. I shared how I loved drawing and making up silly stories, and others talked about their hobbies and interests.

Then, Mrs. Jenkins introduced a fun game called "Walk in My Shoes." She gave us different scenarios, like what it feels like to be the new kid or when someone doesn't understand you. We took turns pretending to be in someone else's shoes, and it was eye-opening! I realized that even though we're all different, we all have feelings and experiences that matter.

The best part was when Mrs. Jenkins brought out a giant puzzle with missing pieces. Each missing piece had a word on it – things like "kindness," "listening," and "patience." She explained that our challenge was to find those missing pieces by showing these qualities to each other.

Armed with our puzzle pieces and the lessons from our puzzle hunt, we worked together to fill in the gaps. We practiced listening when someone spoke, being patient when things got tricky, and showing kindness in everything we did. Our puzzle pieces were magic tools, helping us become even better friends.

As we completed the puzzle, something unique happened – the classroom buzzed with positive vibes. We all felt a more robust connection like we were part of something special. And you know what? The puzzle pieces we found during our hunt fit perfectly into the Friendship Workshop puzzle. It was like our journey was coming full circle.

After the workshop, we looked at each other with big smiles. We realized that true friendship isn't just about finding friends; it's about being a good friend, too. Our puzzle pieces symbolized the incredible friends we were becoming, and I couldn't wait to see what other adventures awaited us on this amazing journey of friendship.

Chapter 6: The Missing Pieces

After our Friendship Workshop, our group was feeling awesome. We had this incredible bond, and our puzzle pieces were like symbols of the amazing friends we were becoming. But you know what they say – no adventure is complete without a few twists and turns.

One day, as we were getting ready for our next puzzle hunt, we realized something shocking – some of our puzzle pieces were missing! It was like a mystery. How could this happen? We'd been so careful with them!

After some detective work, we discovered the pieces were scattered around the school. It was like they'd decided to go on their own little adventure. Instead of feeling upset, we decided to turn it into a challenge – The Great Puzzle Piece Hunt!

Excitedly, we spread out across the school, following clues and using our teamwork skills from our previous adventures. It was a race against time, and every puzzle piece we found felt like a small victory. We even discovered new places in our school we never knew existed!

As we collected the missing pieces, we noticed something cool – each piece had a new word on it. Words like "forgiveness," "flexibility," and "gratitude." The puzzle was evolving, teaching us more about what it takes to be great friends.

Our adventure brought us face-to-face with challenges. At one point, we had to work together to reach a puzzle piece stuck on a high shelf. We used our problem-solving skills and teamwork to create a human ladder, which worked! We cheered and high-fived, feeling a sense of accomplishment.

We gathered all the missing pieces and realized our puzzle had become more beautiful and meaningful. The missing pieces taught us valuable lessons about forgiveness when someone makes a mistake, being flexible when things don't go as planned, and showing gratitude for the friends we have.

Our journey continued, and we knew that even if more challenges came our way, our friendship was strong enough to handle anything. With our puzzle pieces in hand, we looked ahead to new adventures, more laughter, and the excitement of discovering the following chapters of our incredible journey.

Chapter 7: The Grand Finale

After the thrilling Great Puzzle Piece Hunt, our friendship group felt tighter than ever. Our puzzle had transformed into a masterpiece, filled with words like "forgiveness," "flexibility," and "gratitude." We were ready for the grand finale – the moment we'd been waiting for since we found that very first puzzle piece.

Our school decided to host a Friendship Celebration, and we were asked to showcase our puzzle. Excitement bubbled inside me as we carefully arranged our puzzle pieces, creating a beautiful display that told the story of our incredible journey. The whole school gathered for the celebration, and our friends proudly shared their experiences from our adventures. We explained how each puzzle piece taught us something new about friendship, and the crowd listened with smiles and nods of understanding.

As we stood there, presenting our puzzle, I looked at the faces in the audience. I saw kids who used to play alone on the playground, others who felt shy in class, and some who were once scared of being different. Our puzzle had brought us together, and now it inspired others to see the magic of true friendship.

The grand finale came when our principal, Mrs. Turner, handed us a particular puzzle piece. These pieces symbolized our unique contributions to the puzzle of friendship. Mrs. Turner praised our teamwork, kindness, and the way we embraced our differences. Holding my puzzle piece, I felt a warm glow of pride.

The celebration wasn't just about us – it was about everyone in the school recognizing the importance of friendship. We danced, laughed, and celebrated, knowing that our puzzle had become a symbol of unity and understanding.

As the Friendship Celebration ended, we looked at our completed puzzle. It was a masterpiece, not just because of its vibrant colors and intricate design but because it represented the strength of our friendships. The puzzle had started with a single piece, and now it was a beautiful mosaic, each part essential to the whole.
With a heart full of gratitude, I looked at my friends. We had come a long way since I found that first mysterious puzzle piece. Our journey wasn't just a quest for friendship but a lesson in acceptance, kindness, and the incredible power of unity.

Little did we know that our adventure was far from over. The grand finale was the beginning of more laughter, challenges, and the everlasting joy of having each other as friends. As we left the celebration, our puzzle pieces clutched in our hands; we looked forward to the endless possibilities of our friendship-filled future.

After the Friendship Celebration, our school felt like the friendliest place on the planet. The puzzle had worked its magic, bringing everyone closer together. But when we thought our adventure was slowing down, we discovered a new layer to our friendship journey – celebrating our differences.

One day, during recess, we noticed something special happening. Kids from different grades and backgrounds were coming together, forming little groups of their own. It was like the whole school caught the friendship bug, and we were thrilled to see our puzzle's influence spreading.

Our group, with our trusty puzzle pieces, decided to take things up a notch. We organized a "Diversity Day" where everyone could showcase their unique talents, hobbies, and cultures. It was a day to celebrate what made each of us unique.

The preparations were a blast! We brainstormed ideas for the event, made colorful posters, and created a special section for each person to display their uniqueness. I loved how our puzzle pieces had taught us to appreciate differences, and now we were sharing that lesson with the entire school.

When Diversity Day arrived, the excitement was palpable. Students proudly displayed their hobbies, from drawing and playing musical instruments to sharing stories about family traditions. The school courtyard buzzed with laughter and a sense of togetherness.

Our group performed a little skit about our friendship adventure, emphasizing how our differences had made our friendship even more impressive. As we spoke, I could see kids in the audience nodding, realizing that being different wasn't just okay – it was fantastic.
The best part was the Friendship Tree we created. Each student contributed a leaf with their name and something unique about themselves. It symbolizes our collective strength and the beauty of embracing our differences.

During the day, I met kids I'd never spoken to before. We shared stories, laughed together, and discovered that, despite our differences, we had so much in common. It was like our puzzle pieces had sprinkled some magic over the school, creating connections and friendships that bloomed unexpectedly.

As the sun set on Diversity Day, I saw smiles on every face. Our puzzle adventure had evolved into celebrating what made us all special, and it felt incredible. Little did we know that our journey was leaving a lasting impact, teaching our school that true friendship knows no boundaries and that celebrating differences makes our world a more vibrant and joyful place.

Chapter 9: Friendship Forever

Our journey through Diversity Day had left our school buzzing with a new sense of togetherness. The magic of our puzzle adventure had spread, creating an atmosphere of acceptance and joy. But there was still one more chapter to write in our friendship story.

As the weeks passed, our group found new ways to nurture our bonds. We decided to start a Friendship Club, where kids could share stories, play games, and enjoy each other's company. Our puzzle pieces were like honorary members, reminding us of the lessons we'd learned and the incredible friendships we'd formed.

In the Friendship Club, we continued to celebrate our differences. Every week, a different member was the "Friend of the Day," sharing something unique about themselves. Seeing how our unique qualities brought us closer and made our friendships even more meaningful.

One day, we had a brainstorming session for our next big project. We decided to create a mural showcasing the beauty of friendship and diversity. Each member of the Friendship Club would contribute a piece, making it a visual representation of our unity.

The mural day was filled with laughter and teamwork. Each stroke of the paintbrush carried a message of friendship, acceptance, and the importance of celebrating what makes us unique. As the mural took shape, it became a masterpiece that told the story of our incredible journey.

During our Friendship Club meetings, we continued to learn from each other. We discovered new hobbies, shared our dreams, and supported one another through challenges. Though no longer physical objects, our puzzle pieces remained a powerful symbol of the bond we'd created.

Our Friendship Club organized a special Friendship Day as the school year ended. It was a day of games, laughter, and reflections on the fantastic year we'd shared. We looked at our mural, now displayed prominently in the school hallway, and felt a sense of pride. Our friendship story had become a part of the school's history, a reminder that true friendships last a lifetime.

Friendship Club had turned into a family of its own, and as we hugged goodbye on the last day of school, we knew our journey was far from over. Our friendships were like the most treasured stories – they would continue to unfold with each passing day. Little did we know that the next chapter awaited us in the adventures of summer and the many more exciting tales we would create together. Our puzzle adventure had left an everlasting mark on our hearts, a reminder that true friendship is a gift that lasts forever.

As the summer sun warmed our days, I couldn't help but reflect on our Friendship Club's incredible journey. The lessons learned, the friendships formed, and the joy we shared lingered in my heart. Little did I know that the final chapter of our adventure was about to unfold in the most unexpected way.

One sunny afternoon, I received a surprise invitation from Mrs. Jenkins. She wanted me to share our Friendship Club's story at the school assembly. My heart raced with excitement and a touch of nervousness. Standing before the entire school and sharing our journey was a big responsibility.

As I approached the stage, I glanced at our mural displayed in the hallway. It reminded me of our unique friendships, the challenges we overcame, and the beauty that emerged from celebrating our differences. Armed with our puzzle pieces, now transformed into a necklace I wore with pride, I took a deep breath and began sharing our adventure.

I spoke about the first mysterious puzzle piece, our Great Puzzle Piece Hunt, the Friendship Workshop, and the grand finale of the Friendship Celebration. The audience listened intently, and I could feel the magic of our story touching everyone's hearts.

But the most unexpected part of the assembly was yet to come. As I finished sharing our journey, Mrs. Jenkins surprised me with a special guest – a new student named Lily, who had recently joined our school. Lily had been listening backstage and felt inspired by our story.

With a shy smile, Lily joined me on stage. She shared how our Friendship Club's story had encouraged her to embrace her uniqueness and feel confident about making new friends. It was like our adventure had a ripple effect, spreading the magic of friendship to others.
As Lily spoke, I realized the true power of our puzzle adventure. It wasn't just about our group but about creating a school culture of acceptance, kindness, and unity. I learned friendship wasn't limited to the friends we made within our circle; it extended to everyone around us.

The assembly ended with applause, and Lily and I walked off the stagehand in hand. Our Friendship Club had left an impact beyond our close-knit group, connecting us with the entire school community.

As the school year ended, I looked around at the smiling faces, the laughter, and the friendships that had blossomed. Our puzzle adventure taught me the most important lesson – that the true magic of friendship lies in the way it can touch and change the lives of those around us.

I hugged my friends as summer vacation began, knowing our journey had just begun. Our puzzle pieces, now worn by each member of the Friendship Club, served as reminders of the incredible year we had shared. The final chapter had unfolded, leaving us with the promise of more adventures, laughter, and everlasting friendships in the years to come. The lessons learned, the bonds formed, and the joy experienced were the true treasures of our friendship story, a tale that would live on in our hearts forever.

~The End ~

About The Author

Hello, I'm Sharika Pruitt, and I proudly call Birmingham, Alabama my hometown. With over a decade of experience as a licensed mental health professional, I've dedicated myself to helping others navigate the complexities of mental illness and cognitive disabilities. My journey into writing children's books began out of a personal struggle—I couldn't find enough resources for children facing mental, emotional, and learning challenges. Determined to fill this gap, I've poured my heart and soul into creating stories that address these important topics.

My debut book is just the beginning of what I hope will be a series of meaningful works. Through my writing, I aim to shed light on the difficulties children with ADHD and other cognitive disorders face, particularly in forming friendships and social connections. As a Licensed Counselor, I'm thrilled to provide literature that encourages positive socialization skills for children with ADHD. I'm excited about this journey and eager to see where it takes me. Each project is an opportunity to make a difference in the lives of children, and I can't wait to continue this important work.

~With Love,
Sharika N. Pruitt, LPC, NCC
Nationally Recognized Licensed Professional Counselor
www.crossroadstopathwaysllc.com